Mercury HeartLink
www.heartlink.com

HolyFunk

HolyFunk

polaroids & poems

Kim Nuzzo

HolyFunk: polaroids and poems
Copyright ©2012 Kim Nuzzo

ISBN: 978-0-9854153-5-8
Publisher: Mercury HeartLink
Printed in the United States of America

Book design by Mercury HeartLink, *www.heartlink.com*

contact Kim Nuzo at: knuzzo3@gmail.com

_____

"The author would like to recognize the significant role
played by his publisher, Stewart Warren of Mercury HeartLink,
more creative shaman than technician, who brought out
whatever was necessary to serve the art." —KN

Introduction

Somewhere out in the Midwest, near the Mississippi River banks of my origins, I dreamt of a den where crow boys like us played in the Theater of the Absurd, deep underground. The blazing blue sky far above us. In our burrow, the best sky was still in B&W. . . and emerged like bats from a cave. . . you could feel the disturbed air from those unexpected openings. As we laughed, slapstick colors were imagined.

Often when I visited him in his apt. in Madison, WI, he would pop a few exposed Polaroid's into a warm oven, instead of dessert muffins. . . & we would squish the soft pigment around to our delight. Then prop them up on the table & write a free form poetic word-play response.

We worshiped Space Tadpole, a creature able to leap the paradoxical extremes, yet remain heroic & entered into a lifelong collaboration that will only end when one of us is dead. . . & I'm not sure if even then.

Kim took me to magical places. . . like the Valley of Lights. . . in the hilly driftless area of Wisc. where the glassier slid around us. He's a wilder-than-life photographer & a renegade word bounty hunter. (I can only imagine what he would have fondled had he not been kicked out of seminary school). He had pelts in his belt. . . and seized the moment like a farmer beheads his chickens, then watching them run about, without thoughts. . .

He told me he wants to hike to Delicate Arch in Utah once every day for a year. . . 365 days in a row. . . a kind of a performance ritual. He gets these extreme ideas from time to time. I say, good luck starboy. . . I'm sleeping in. I'll wonder where ya went to at 4:00 in the morning. . . & imagine you walking through that Elysian archway when I am awake in my dream.

—Ron Byers, 2012

dedicated to

Love

my three *illuminati*

Gentian, Laurel and Gina

Redux believes above all in pont-consciousness, the leaping between disparate things, ideas, sensory moments so that new arcs and dynamics of relationship (and disrelationship) may form.

—Joe Weil, Redux, A Manifesto

I

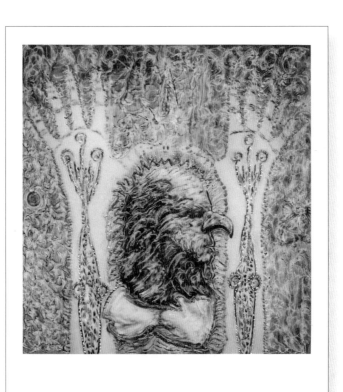

in a temple of dreams

in the soft seeing flesh

i am only here now, secretly,

briefly

forgive my dreams their deep desire

something deeper grows

like an old soul

this time so much sadness

_____

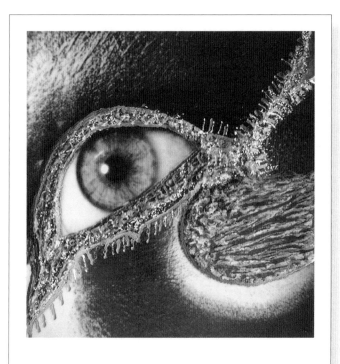

the god i saw was not the god

the god i saw was whirling

starry ideas

bouquets of hallelujahs

_____

mysterious uncertainties play

wonder, prayers, sanctuary

———————————

II

———————————————————

a broken bruised sky

an angel temporarily living in hell

_____

he swims through the air with heaven inside

like a golden word

like nothing on earth

is he even real

he stands alone

on the shore of a small death

———————

the deep dream resurrects

———————————————

no other world

blue mantra of the moment

_____

beyond the last incarnation

a prize of clouds

hydrogen thoughts

one day, he whispers

his secret testimony to the white silence

_____

after,

he will always see her

smiling in an empty doorway

salt and blood

all there was

I have a big sky

soon we'll be mingled with dust

_____

And

the gardeners of the present moment

gatherers of clarities

_____

_____

milky dawns of paradise

in the great vibrating blessedness

it will look like sunflowers on fire

we will not have a name for it

with his bruised palms

with his shaman hands

_____

in unmarked space

rosy blameless vision

at the mystical edge of dreams

one, hot-blooded flash

———

inside the nucleus of our sweet

bitter

wonder

grace is important here

in the exquisite pain

of the aching restless road

———————————————————

the lost and the fallen

of passion, the strange

poem of it all

he doesn't know

he has a heart

he smiles

to feel his sadness

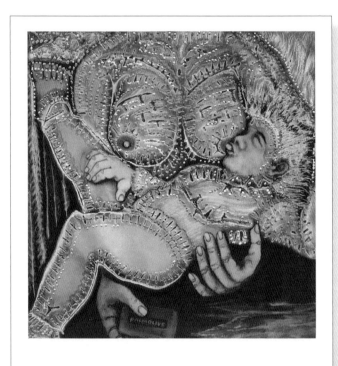

This is a love poem.

It is curious.

_____

_____

open the door

and let the sun soften you

broken perceptions

of the unnamed soul

we won't have a name for it

it will awaken the light

I dream countless versions of myself

as wide as the land of milk and honey

———————————————

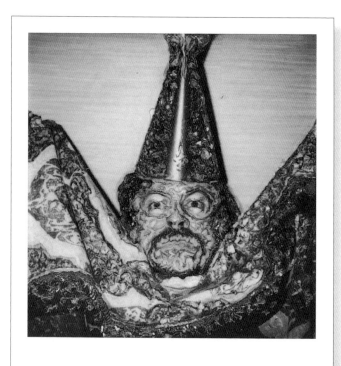

count the crow hours and days

we can call it a gift

_____

III

---

in pain of evolution

a simmering, brilliant spasm

_____

meaning shifts as things

fall apart

pretend an invincible show

wait for the stars to be just right

_____

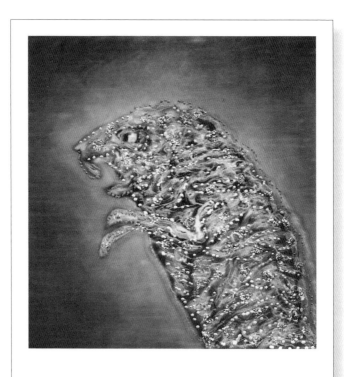

secret testimony to the white silence

he whispers

in articulate pulses of communion

through unmapped spaces

───────────────────────

---

a wonder under scars

Amen and Salvation down in the guts of a soul

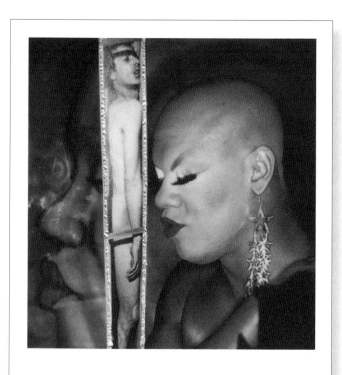

all moments of immense contradiction

you bless me

_____

in one hot-blooded flash

seeking to be found

That is why the contemplative person, without ever leaving his village, will nevertheless have the whole universe at his disposal. There's infinity in a cell or a desert. One can sleep cosmically against a rock.

—Fernando Pessoa, The Book of Disquiet

About the Author

Kim Nuzzo is a poet, actor and visual artist living in the Roaring Fork Valley of western Colorado. As President of the Aspen Poets' Society he cofounded and hosts Live Poetry Night at Victoria's Espresso and Wine Bar in Aspen. He is currently finishing work on a one man show: *Poets and Outlaws, Mystics and Saints.*

You can follow him at his blog, Aspen Holyfunk at *www.heartofeverything.blogspot.com*

Made in the USA
Charleston, SC
17 May 2014